Harriet Beecher Stowe

Religious Poems

Harriet Beecher Stowe

Religious Poems

ISBN/EAN: 9783337719869

Printed in Europe, USA, Canada, Australia, Japan

Cover: Foto ©Lupo / pixelio.de

More available books at **www.hansebooks.com**

RELIGIOUS POEMS.

BY

HARRIET BEECHER STOWE.

WITH ILLUSTRATIONS.

BOSTON:
TICKNOR AND FIELDS.
1867.

Entered according to Act of Congress, in the year 1867, by
HARRIET BEECHER STOWE,
in the Clerk's Office of the District Court of the District of Massachusetts.

UNIVERSITY PRESS: WELCH, BIGELOW, & CO.,
CAMBRIDGE.

CONTENTS.

	PAGE
St. Catherine borne by Angels	1
The Charmer	6
Knocking	10
The Old Psalm Tune	15
The Other World	19
Mary at the Cross	22
The Inner Voice	28
Abide in me, and I in you	30
The Secret	32
Think not all is over	34
Lines to the Memory of "Annie"	36
The Crocus	39
Consolation	41
"Only a Year"	44
Below	47
Above	49
Lines on the Death of Mrs. Stuart	53
Summer Studies	57

Hours of the Night.

    I. Midnight 65
    II. First Hour . . . 68
    III. Second Hour 71
    IV. Third Hour . . 74
    V. Fourth Hour . . 77
    VI. Day Dawn 85
    VII. When I awake I am still with Thee . 88

Pressed Flowers from Italy.

    A Day in the Pamfili Doria . . . 93
    The Gardens of the Vatican . 102
    St. Peter's Church . . 104
    The Miserere 106

ST. CATHERINE BORNE BY ANGELS.*

SLOW through the solemn air, in silence sailing,
   Borne by mysterious angels, strong and fair,
She sleeps at last, blest dreams her eyelids veiling,
   Above this weary world of strife and care.

---

* According to this legend, Catherine was a noble maiden of Alexandria, distinguished alike by birth, riches, beauty, and the rarest gifts of genius and learning. In the flower of her life she consecrated herself to the service of her Redeemer, and cheerfully suffered for his sake the loss of wealth, friends, and the esteem of the world. Banishment, imprisonment,

Lo how she passeth!—dreamy, slow, and calm:
  Scarce wave those broad, white wings, so silvery
      bright;
Those cloudy robes, in star-emblazoned folding,
  Sweep mistily athwart the evening light.

Far, far below, the dim, forsaken earth,
  The foes that threaten, or the friends that weep;
Past, like a dream, the torture and the pain:
  For so He giveth his beloved sleep.

The restless bosom of the surging ocean
  Gives back the image as the cloud floats o'er,
Hushing in glassy awe his troubled motion;
  For one blest moment he complains no more.

and torture were in vain tried to shake the constancy of her faith; and at last she was bound upon the torturing-wheel for a cruel death. But the angels descended, so says the story, rent the wheel, and bore her away, through the air, far over the sea, to Mount Sinai, where her body was left to repose, and her soul ascended with them to heaven.

St. Catherine borne by Angels

Like the transparent golden floor of heaven,
  His charmed waters lie as in a dream,
And glistening wings, and starry robes unfolding,
  And serious angel eyes far downward gleam.

O restless sea! thou seemest all enchanted
  By that sweet vision of celestial rest;
Where are the winds and tides thy peace that haunted, —
  So still thou seemest, so glorified and blest!

Ah, sea! to-morrow, that sweet scene forgotten,
  Dark tides and tempests shall thy bosom rear;
And thy complaining waves, with restless motion,
  Shall toss their hands in their old wild despair.

So o'er our hearts sometimes the sweet, sad story
  Of suffering saints, borne homeward crowned and blest,
Shines down in stillness with a tender glory,
  And makes a mirror there of breathless rest.

For not alone in those old Eastern regions
  Are Christ's beloved ones tried by cross and
    chain ;
In many a house are his elect ones hidden,
  His martyrs suffering in their patient pain.

The rack, the cross, life's weary wrench of woe,
  The world sees not, as slow, from day to day,
In calm, unspoken patience, sadly still,
  The loving spirit bleeds itself away.

But there are hours when, from the heavens unfold-
    ing,
  Come down the angels with the glad release ;
And we look upward, to behold in glory
  Our suffering loved ones borne away to peace.

Ah, brief the calm ! the restless wave of feeling
  Rises again when the bright cloud sweeps by,
And our unrestful souls reflect no longer
  That tender vision of the upper sky.

St. Catherine borne by Angels.

Espoused Lord of the pure saints in glory,
 To whom all faithful souls affianced are,
Breathe down thy peace into our restless spirits,
 And make a lasting, heavenly vision there.

So the bright gates no more on us shall close;
 No more the cloud of angels fade away;
And we shall walk, amid life's weary strife,
 In the calm light of thine eternal day.

THE CHARMER.

"*Socrates.* However, you and Simmias appear to me as if you wished to sift this subject more thoroughly, and to be afraid, like children, lest, on the soul's departure from the body, winds should blow it away.

"Upon this Cebes said, 'Endeavor to teach us better, Socrates. Perhaps there is a childish spirit in our breast that has such a dread. Let us endeavor to persuade him not to be afraid of death, as of hobgoblins.'

"'But you must charm him every day,' said Socrates, 'until you have quieted his fears.'

"'But whence, O Socrates,' he said, 'can we procure a skilful charmer for such a case, now you are about to leave us.'

"'Greece is wide, Cebes,' he said, 'and in it surely there are skilful men; and there are many barbarous nations, all of which you should search, seeking such a charmer, sparing neither money nor toil.'" — Last words of Socrates, as narrated by Plato in the *Phædo*.

WE need that charmer, for our hearts are sore
    With longings for the things that may not be,
Faint for the friends that shall return no more,
    Dark with distrust, or wrung with agony.

"What is this life? and what to us is death?
  Whence came we? whither go? and where are
    those
Who, in a moment stricken from our side,
  Passed to that land of shadow and repose?

"And are they all dust? and dust must we become?
  Or are they living in some unknown clime?
Shall we regain them in that far-off home,
  And live anew beyond the waves of time?

"O man divine! on thee our souls have hung:
  Thou wert our teacher in these questions high:
But ah! this day divides thee from our side,
  And veils in dust thy kindly-guiding eye.

"Where is that Charmer whom thou bidst us seek?
  On what far shores may his sweet voice be heard?
When shall these questions of our yearning souls
  Be answered by the bright Eternal Word?"

So spake the youth of Athens, weeping round,
    When Socrates lay calmly down to die ;
So spake the sage, prophetic of the hour
    When earth's fair morning star should rise on high.

They found Him not, those youths of soul divine,
    Long seeking, wandering, watching on life's shore ;
Reasoning, aspiring, yearning for the light,
    Death came and found them—doubting as before.

But years passed on ; and lo! the Charmer came,
    Pure, simple, sweet, as comes the silver dew,
And the world knew him not, — he walked alone,
    Encircled only by his trusting few.

Like the Athenian sage, rejected, scorned,
    Betrayed, condemned, his day of doom drew nigh ;
He drew his faithful few more closely round,
    And told them that his hour was come—to die.

"Let not your heart be troubled," then He said,
  "My Father's house hath mansions large and fair;
I go before you to prepare your place,
  I will return to take you with me there."

And since that hour the awful foe is charmed,
  And life and death are glorified and fair:
Whither He went we know, the way we know,
  And with firm step press on to meet him there.

KNOCKING.

"Behold, I stand at the door and knock."

KNOCKING, knocking, ever knocking?
    Who is there?
"T is a pilgrim, strange and kingly,
    Never such was seen before; —
Ah, sweet soul, for such a wonder
    Undo the door.

No, — that door is hard to open;
Hinges rusty, latch is broken;
    Bid Him go.
Wherefore, with that knocking dreary
Scare the sleep from one so weary?
    Say Him, — no.

Knocking, knocking, ever knocking?
    What! Still there?
O, sweet soul, but once behold Him,
With the glory-crownéd hair;
And those eyes, so strange and tender,

Waiting there;
Open! Open! Once behold Him,—
Him, so fair.

Ah, that door! Why wilt Thou vex me,
Coming ever to perplex me?
For the key is stiffly rusty,
And the bolt is clogged and dusty;
Many-fingered ivy-vine
Seals it fast with twist and twine;
Weeds of years and years before
Choke the passage of that door.

Knocking! knocking! What! still knocking?
    He still there?
What's the hour? The night is waning,—
In my heart a drear complaining,
    And a chilly, sad unrest!
Ah, this knocking! It disturbs me,
Scares my sleep with dreams unblest!

Give me rest,
Rest, — ah, rest!

Rest, dear soul, He longs to **give thee**;
Thou hast only dreamed **of** pleasure,
Dreamed of gifts and golden treasure,
Dreamed of jewels in thy keeping,
Waked to weariness of weeping; —
Open to thy soul's one Lover,
And thy night **of** dreams is over, —
The true gifts He **brings have seeming**
More than all thy faded dreaming!

Did she open? **Doth she?** Will she?
So, **as** wondering **we behold,**
Grows the picture to a sign,
Pressed upon your soul **and** mine;
For in every **breast** that liveth
Is that strange mysterious **door**; —

Though forsaken and betangled,
Ivy-gnarled and weed-bejangled,
Dusty, rusty, and forgotten ; —
There the piercéd hand still knocketh,
And with ever-patient watching,
With the sad eyes true and tender,
With the glory-crownéd hair, —
Still a God is waiting there.

THE OLD PSALM TUNE.

YOU asked, dear friend, the other day,
    Why still my charmèd ear
Rejoiceth in uncultured tone
    That old psalm tune to hear?

I've heard full oft, in foreign lands,
    The grand orchestral strain,
Where music's ancient masters live,
    Revealed on earth again, —

Where breathing, solemn instruments,
    In swaying clouds of sound,
Bore up the yearning, trancéd soul,
    Like silver wings around; —

I've heard in old St. Peter's dome,
  Where clouds of incense rise,
Most ravishing the choral swell
  Mount upwards to the skies.

And well I feel the magic power,
  When skilled and cultured art
Its cunning webs of sweetness weaves
  Around the captured heart.

But yet, dear friend, though rudely sung,
  That old psalm tune hath still
A pulse of power beyond them all
  My inmost soul to thrill.

Those halting tones that sound to you,
  Are not the tones I hear;
But voices of the loved and lost
  There meet my longing ear.

I hear **my** angel mother's voice, —
    Those were the words she sung;
I hear my brother's ringing **tones**,
    As once on earth they rung;

And friends that walk in **white above**
    Come round me like **a cloud,**
And far above those earthly notes
    Their singing sounds aloud.

There may **be** discord, **as you say**;
    Those voices poorly ring;
But there's no discord in the strain
    Those upper **spirits** sing.

For they who sing **are of the blest,**
    The calm and glorified,
Whose hours are one eternal rest
    On heaven's sweet floating tide.

Their life is music and accord ;
    Their souls and hearts keep time
In one sweet concert with the Lord, —
    One concert vast, sublime.

And through the hymns they sang on earth
    Sometimes a sweetness falls
On those they loved and left below,
    And softly homeward calls, —

Bells from our own dear fatherland,
    Borne trembling o'er the sea, —
The narrow sea that they have crossed,
    The shores where we shall be.

O sing, sing on, beloved souls !
    Sing cares and griefs to rest :
Sing, till entrancèd we arise
    To join you 'mong the blest.

THE OTHER WORLD.

It lies around us like a cloud,
  A world we do not see;
Yet the sweet closing of an eye
  May bring us there to be.

Its gentle breezes fan our cheek,
  Amid our worldly cares,
Its gentle voices whisper love,
  And mingle with our prayers.

Sweet hearts around us throb and beat,
  Sweet helping hands are stirred,
And palpitates the veil between
  With breathings almost heard.

The silence, awful, sweet, and calm,
    They have no power to break ;
For mortal words are not for them
    To utter or partake.

So thin, so soft, so sweet, they glide,
    So near to press they seem,
They lull us gently to our rest,
    They melt into our dream.

And in the hush of rest they bring
    'T is easy now to see
How lovely and how sweet a pass
    The hour of death may be ; —

To close the eye, and close the ear,
    Wrapped in a trance of bliss,
And, gently drawn in loving arms,
    To swoon to that — from this, —

The Other World.

Scarce knowing if we wake or sleep,
   Scarce asking where we are,
To feel all evil sink away,
   All sorrow and all care.

Sweet souls around us! watch us still;
   Press nearer to our side;
Into our thoughts, into our prayers,
   With gentle helpings glide.

Let death between us be as naught,
   A dried and vanished stream;
Your joy be the reality,
   Our suffering life the dream.

MARY AT THE CROSS.

"Now there stood by the cross of Jesus his mother."

O WONDROUS mother! since the dawn of time
    Was ever love, was ever grief, like thine?
O highly favored in thy joy's deep flow,
    And favored, even in this, thy bitterest woe!

Poor was that home in simple Nazareth
    Where, fairly growing, like some silent flower,
Last of a kingly race, unknown and lowly,
    O desert lily, passed thy childhood's hour.

The world knew not the tender, serious maiden,
    Who through deep loving years so silent grew,

Mary at the Cross.

Full of high thought and holy aspiration,
    Which the o'ershadowing God alone might view.

And then it came, that message from the highest,
    Such as to woman ne'er before descended,
The almighty wings thy prayerful soul o'erspread,
    And with thy life the Life of worlds was blended.

What visions then of future glory filled thee,
    The chosen mother of that King unknown,
Mother fulfiller of all prophecy
    Which, through dim ages, wondering seers had shown!

Well did thy dark eye kindle, thy deep soul
    Rise into billows, and thy heart rejoice;
Then woke the poet's fire, the prophet's song,
    Tuned with strange burning words thy timid voice.

Then, in dark contrast, came the lowly manger,
    The outcast shed, the tramp of brutal feet;
Again behold earth's learned and her lowly,
    Sages and shepherds, prostrate at thy feet.

Then to the temple bearing — hark again
    What strange conflicting tones of prophecy
Breathe o'er the child foreshadowing words of joy,
    High triumph blent with bitter agony!

Mary at the Cross.

O, highly favored thou in many an hour
   Spent in lone musings with thy wondrous Son,
When thou didst gaze into that glorious eye,
   And hold that mighty hand within thine **own**.

Blest through those thirty **years,** when **in** thy
      dwelling
   He lived **a** God disguised with unknown power;
And thou his sole **adorer, his best love,**
   Trusting, **revering, waited for his hour.**

Blest in that hour, when called by opening heaven
   With cloud and voice, and the baptizing flame,
Up from the Jordan walked **th'** acknowledged
      stranger,
   And **awe-struck crowds grew silent as he** came.

Blessed, when **full of grace, with** glory crowned,
   He from both hands almighty favors poured,

And, though He had not where to lay his head,
    Brought to his feet alike the slave and lord.

Crowds followed ; thousands shouted, " Lo, our
    King ! "
    Fast beat thy heart. Now, now the hour draws
        nigh :
Behold the crown, the throne, the nations bend !
    Ah, no ! fond mother, no ! behold him die !

Now by that cross thou tak'st thy final station,
    And shar'st the last dark trial of thy Son ;
Not with weak tears or woman's lamentation,
    But with high, silent anguish, like his own.

Hail ! highly favored, even in this deep passion ;
    Hail ! in this bitter anguish thou art blest, —
Blest in the holy power with Him to suffer
    Those deep death-pangs that lead to higher rest.

All now is darkness; and in that deep stillness
   The God-man wrestles with that mighty woe;
Hark to that cry, the rock of ages rending, —
   "'T is finished!" Mother, all is glory now!

By sufferings mighty as his mighty soul
   Hath the Redeemer risen forever blest;
And through all ages must his heart-beloved
   Through the same baptism enter the same rest.

THE INNER VOICE.

"Come ye yourselves into a desert place and rest awhile; for there were many coming and going, so that they had no time so much as to eat."

'MID the mad whirl of life, its dim confusion,
   Its jarring discords and poor vanity,
Breathing like music over troubled waters,
   What gentle voice, O Christian, speaks to thee?

It is a stranger, — not of earth or earthly;
   By the serene, deep fulness of that eye, —
By the calm, pitying smile, the gesture lowly, —
   It is thy Saviour as he passeth by.

"Come, come," he saith, "O soul oppressed and weary,
   Come to the shadows of my desert rest,

Come walk with me far from life's babbling discords,
    And peace shall breathe like music in thy breast.

"Art thou bewildered by contesting voices, —
    Sick to thy soul of party noise and strife?
Come, leave it all, and seek that solitude
    Where thou shalt learn of me a purer life.

"When far behind the world's great tumult dieth,
    Thou shalt look back and wonder at its roar;
But its far voice shall seem to thee a dream,
    Its power to vex thy holier life be o'er.

"There shalt thou learn the secret of a power,
    Mine to bestow, which heals the ills of living:
To overcome by love, to live by prayer,
    To conquer man's worst evils by forgiving."

ABIDE IN ME, AND I IN YOU.

THE SOUL'S ANSWER.

THAT mystic word of thine, O sovereign Lord,
   Is all too pure, too high, too deep for me;
Weary of striving, and with longing faint,
   I breathe it back again in *prayer* to thee.

Abide in me, I pray, and I in thee;
   From this good hour, O, leave me nevermore;
Then shall the discord cease, the wound be healed,
   The lifelong bleeding of the soul be o'er.

Abide in me; o'ershadow by thy love
   Each half-formed purpose and dark thought of sin;

Quench, e'er it rise, each selfish, low desire,
    And keep my soul as thine, calm and divine.

As some rare perfume in a vase of clay
    Pervades it with a fragrance not its own,
So, when thou dwellest in a mortal soul,
    All heaven's own sweetness seems around it thrown.

Abide in me: there have been moments blest
    When I have heard thy voice and felt thy power;
Then evil lost its grasp, and passion, hushed,
    Owned the divine enchantment of the hour.

These were but seasons, beautiful and rare;
    Abide in me, and they shall ever be.
Fulfil at once thy precept and my prayer,—
    Come, and abide in me, and I in thee.

THE SECRET.

"Thou shalt keep them in the secret of thy presence from the strife of tongues."

WHEN winds are raging o'er the upper ocean,
    And billows wild contend with angry roar,
'Tis said, far down beneath the wild commotion,
    That peaceful stillness reigneth evermore.

Far, far beneath, the noise of tempest dieth,
    And silver waves chime ever peacefully;
And no rude storm, how fierce soe'er he flieth,
    Disturbs the sabbath of that deeper sea.

So to the soul that knows thy love, O Purest,
    There is a temple peaceful evermore!
And all the babble of life's angry voices
    Die in hushed stillness at its sacred door.

The Secret.

Far, far away the noise of passion dieth,
    And loving thoughts rise ever peacefully;
And no rude storm, how fierce soe'er he **flieth**,
    Disturbs that deeper rest, O Lord, in thee.

O rest of rests! O peace serene, eternal!
    Thou ever livest **and** thou changest **never**;
And in the secret of thy presence dwelleth
    Fulness of joy, forever and forever.

THINK NOT ALL IS OVER.

THINK not, when the wailing winds of autumn
    Drive the shivering leaflets from the tree, —
Think not all is over: spring returneth,
Buds and leaves and blossoms thou shalt see.

Think not, when the earth lies cold and sealed,
And the weary birds above her mourn, —
Think not all is over: God still liveth,
Songs and sunshine shall again return.

Think not, when thy heart is waste and dreary,
When thy cherished hopes lie chill and sere, —
Think not all is over: God still loveth,
He will wipe away thy every tear.

Think not all is over.

Weeping for a night alone endureth,
God at last shall bring a morning hour;
In the frozen buds of every winter
Sleep the blossoms of a future flower.

LINES

**TO THE MEMORY OF "ANNIE," WHO DIED AT MILAN,
JUNE 6, 1860.**

"Jesus saith unto her, Woman, why weepest thou? whom seekest thou? She, supposing him to be the gardener, saith unto him, Sir, if thou have borne him hence, tell me where thou hast laid him."— JOHN xx. 15.

IN the fair gardens of celestial peace
   Walketh a Gardener in meekness clad;
Fair are the flowers that wreathe his dewy locks,
   And his mysterious eyes are sweet and sad.

Fair are the silent foldings of his robes,
   Falling with saintly calmness to his feet;
And when he walks, each floweret to his will
   With living pulse of sweet accord doth beat.

Every green leaf thrills to its tender heart,
   In the mild summer radiance of his eye;

No fear of storm, **or** cold, **or** bitter frost,
   Shadows the flowerets when their sun **is nigh.**

And all our pleasant haunts of earthly love
   Are nurseries to those gardens of the **air** ;
And his far-darting eye, with starry beam,
   Watcheth the growing of his treasures there.

We call them ours, o'erwept with selfish tears,
   O'erwatched with restless longings night and day;
Forgetful of the high, mysterious right
   He holds to bear our cherished plants away.

But when some sunny spot in those bright **fields**
   Needs the fair presence of an added flower,
Down sweeps a starry angel in the night :
   At morn, the rose has vanished from our bower.

Where **stood** our tree, **our** flower, there is **a grave** !
   Blank, silent, vacant, but in worlds above,

Like a new star outblossomed in the skies,
    The angels hail an added flower of love.

Dear friend, no more upon that lonely mound,
    Strewed with the red and yellow autumn leaf,
Drop thou the tear, but raise the fainting eye
    Beyond the autumn mists of earthly grief.

Thy garden rose-bud bore, within its breast,
    Those mysteries of color, warm and bright,
That the bleak climate of this lower sphere
    Could never waken into form and light.

Yes, the sweet Gardener hath borne her hence,
    Nor must thou ask to take her thence away;
Thou shalt behold her in some coming hour,
    Full-blossomed in his fields of cloudless day.

THE CROCUS.

BENEATH the sunny autumn sky,
   With gold leaves dropping round,
We sought, my little friend and **I**,
   The consecrated ground,
Where, calm beneath the holy cross,
   O'ershadowed by sweet skies,
Sleeps tranquilly that youthful form,
   Those blue unclouded eyes.

Around the soft, green swelling mound
   We scooped the earth away,
And buried deep the crocus-bulbs
   Against a coming day.
" These roots are dry, and brown, and sere:
   Why plant them here?" he said.
" To leave them, all the winter long,
   So desolate and **dead.**"

The Crocus.

"Dear child, within each sere dead form
  There sleeps a living flower,
And angel-like it shall arise
  In spring's returning hour."
Ah, deeper down — cold, dark, and chill —
  We buried our heart's flower,
But angel-like shall he arise
  In spring's immortal hour.

In blue and yellow from its grave
  Springs up the crocus fair,
And God shall raise those bright blue eyes,
  Those sunny waves of hair.
Not for a fading summer's morn,
  Not for a fleeting hour,
But for an endless age of bliss,
  Shall rise our heart's dear flower.

CONSOLATION.

WRITTEN AFTER THE SECOND BATTLE OF BULL RUN.

"And I saw a new heaven and a new earth : for the first heaven and the first earth were passed away ; and there was no more sea."

AH, many-voiced and angry! how the waves
    Beat turbulent with terrible uproar !
Is there no rest from tossing, — no repose ?
    Where shall we find a haven and a shore ?

What is secure from the loud-dashing wave ?
    There go our riches, and our hopes fly there :
There go the faces of our best beloved,
    Whelmed in the vortex of its wild despair.

Whose son is safe? whose brother, and whose home?
    The dashing spray beats out the household fire :
By blackened ashes weep our widowed souls
    Over the embers of our lost desire.

By pauses, in the fitful moaning storm,
  We hear triumphant notes of battle roll.
Too soon the triumph sinks in funeral wail;
  The muffled drum, the death march, shakes the
    soul!

Rocks on all sides, and breakers! at the helm
  Weak human hand and weary human eyes.
The shout and clamor of our dreary strife
  Goes up conflicting to the angry skies.

But for all this, O timid hearts, be strong;
  Be of good cheer, for, though the storm must be,
It hath its Master: from the depths shall rise
  New heavens, new earth, where shall be no more
    sea.

No sea, no tossing, no unrestful storm!
  Forever past the anguish and the strife;
The poor old weary earth shall bloom again,
  With the bright foliage of that better life.

And war, and strife, and hatred, shall be past,
  And misery be a forgotten dream.
The Shepherd God shall lead his peaceful fold
  By the calm meadows and the quiet stream.

Be still, be still, and know that he is God;
  Be calm, be trustful; work, and watch, and pray,
Till from the throes of this last anguish rise
  The light and gladness of that better day.

"ONLY A YEAR."

ONE year ago, — a ringing voice,
    A clear blue eye,
And clustering curls of sunny hair,
    Too fair to die.

Only a year, — no voice, no smile,
    No glance of eye,
No clustering curls of golden hair,
    Fair but to die!

One year ago, — what loves, what schemes
    Far into life!
What joyous hopes, what high resolves,
    What generous strife!

"Only a Year."

The silent picture on the wall,
  The burial stone,
Of all that beauty, **life, and** joy
  Remain **alone!**

One year, — **one** year, — one little year,
  And so much gone!
And yet the even **flow of life**
  Moves calmly **on.**

The grave grows green, the flowers bloom fair,
  Above **that head;**
No sorrowing tint of leaf or spray
  Says he is dead.

No pause or hush of merry **birds,**
  That sing above,
Tells us how coldly sleeps below
  The form we love.

Where hast thou been this year, beloved?
  What hast thou seen?
What visions fair, what glorious life,
  Where thou hast been?

The veil! the veil! so thin, so strong!
  'Twixt us and thee;
The mystic veil! when shall it fall,
  That we may see?

Not dead, not sleeping, not even gone,
  But present still,
And waiting for the coming hour
  Of God's sweet will.

Lord of the living and the dead,
  Our Saviour dear!
We lay in silence at thy feet
  This sad, sad year!

BELOW.

L OUDLY sweep the winds of autumn
   O'er that lone, beloved grave,
Where we laid those sunny ringlets,
When those blue eyes set like stars,
Leaving us to outer darkness.
O the longing and the aching!
O the sere deserted grave!

Let the grass turn brown upon thee,
Brown and withered like our dreams!
Let the wind moan through the pine-trees
With a dreary, dirge-like whistle,
Sweep the dead leaves on its bosom, —
Moaning, sobbing through the branches,
Where the summer laughed so gayly.

He is gone, our boy of summer, —
Gone the light of his blue eyes,
Gone the tender heart and manly,
Gone the dreams and the aspirings, —
Nothing but the *mound* remaineth,
And the aching in our bosoms,
Ever aching, ever throbbing :
Who shall bring it unto rest?

ABOVE.

A VISION.

COMING down a golden street
    I beheld my vanished one,
And he moveth on a cloud,
And his forehead wears a star ;
And his blue eyes, deep and holy,
Fixed as in a blessed dream,
See some mystery of joy,
Some unuttered depth of love.

And his vesture is as blue
As the skies of summer are,
Falling with a saintly sweep,
With a sacred stillness swaying ;
And he presseth to his bosom
Harp of strange and mystic fashion.

And his hands, like living pearls,
Wander o'er the golden strings.

And the music that ariseth,
Who can utter or divine it?
In that strange celestial thrilling,
Every memory of sorrow,
Every heart-ache, every anguish,
Every fear for the to-morrow,
Melt away in charmèd rest.

And there be around him many,
Bright with robes like evening clouds, —
Tender green and clearest amber,
Crimson fading into rose,
Robes of flames and robes of silver, —
And their hues all thrill and tremble
With a living light of feeling,
Deepening with each heart's pulsation,
Till in vivid trance of color
That celestial rainbow glows.

How they float and wreathe and brighten,
Bending low their starry brows,
Singing with a tender cadence,
And their hands, like spotless lilies,
Folded on their prayerful breasts.
In their singing seem to mingle
Tender airs of by-gone days;—
Mother-hymnings by the cradle,
Mother-moanings by the grave,
Songs of human love and sorrow,
Songs of endless love and rest;—
In the pauses of that music
Every throb of sorrow dies.

O my own, my heart's belovéd,
Vainly have I wept above thee?
Would I call thee from thy glory
To this world's impurity?—
Lo! it passeth, it dissolveth,
All the vision melts away;

But as if a heavenly lily
Dropped into my aching breast,
With a healing sweetness laden,
With a mystic breath of rest,
I am charmed into forgetting
Autumn winds and dreary grave.

LINES

SUGGESTED BY THE DEATH OF MRS. PROFESSOR STUART
OF ANDOVER, MASS.

How quiet, through the hazy autumn air,
 The elm-boughs wave with many a gold-
  flecked leaf!
How calmly float the dreamy mantled clouds
Through these still days of autumn, fair and brief!

Our Andover stands thoughtful, fair, and calm,
Waiting to lay her summer glories by
E'er the bright flush shall kindle all her pines,
And her woods blaze with autumn's heraldry.

By the old mossy wall the golden-rod
Waves as aforetime, and the purple sprays
Of starry asters quiver to the breeze,
Rustling all stilly through the forest ways.

No voice of triumph from those silent skies
Breaks on the calm, and speaks of glories near,
Nor bright wings flutter, nor fair glistening robes
Proclaim that heavenly messengers are here.

Yet in our midst an angel hath come down,
Troubling the waters in a peaceful home;
And from that home, of life's long sickness healed,
A saint hath risen, where pain no more may come.

Christ's fair elect one, from a hidden life
Of loving deeds and words of gentleness,
Hath passed where all are loving and beloved,
Beyond all weariness and all distress.

Calm, like a lamb in shepherd's bosom borne,
Quiet and trustful hath she sunk to rest;
God breathed in tenderness the sweet "Well done!"
That scarce awoke a trance so still and blest.

Lines.

Ye who remember the long loving years,
The patient mother's hourly martyrdom,
The self-renouncing wisdom, the calm trust,
Rejoice for her whose day of rest is come!

Father and mother, now united, stand
Waiting for you to bind the household chain;
The tent is struck, the home is gone before,
And tarries for you on the heavenly plain.

By every wish repressed and hope resigned,
Each cross accepted and each sorrow borne,
She dead yet speaketh, she doth beckon you
To tread the path her patient feet have worn.

Each year that world grows richer and more dear
With the bright freight washed from life's stormy
    shore;
O goodly clime, how lovely is thy strand,
With those dear faces seen on earth no more!

The veil between this world and that to come
Grows tremulous and quivers with their breath ;
Dimly we hear their voices, see their hands,
Inviting us to the release of death.

O Thou, in whom thy saints above, below,
Are one and undivided, grant us grace
In patience yet to bear our daily cross, —
In patience run our hourly shortening race !

And while on earth we wear the servant's form,
And while life's labors ever toilful be,
Breathe in our souls the joyful confidence
We are already kings and priests with thee.

SUMMER STUDIES.

WHY shouldst thou study in the month of June
In dusky books of Greek and Hebrew lore,
When the Great Teacher of all glorious things
Passes in hourly light before thy door?

There is a brighter book unrolling now;
Fair are its leaves as is the tree of heaven,
All veined and dewed and gemmed with wondrous signs,
To which a healing mystic power is given.

A thousand voices to its study call,
From the fair hill-top, from the waterfall,
Where the bird singeth, and the yellow bee,
And the breeze talketh from the airy tree.

Now is that glorious resurrection time
When all earth's buried beauties have new birth:
Behold the yearly miracle complete, —
God hath created a new heaven and earth!

No tree that wants its joyful garments now,
No flower but hastes his bravery to don;
God bids thee to this marriage feast of joy,
Let thy soul put the wedding garment on.

All fringed with festal gold the barberry stands;
The ferns, exultant, clap their new-made wings:
The hemlock rustles broideries of fresh green,
And thousand bells of pearl the blueberry rings.

The long, weird fingers of the old white-pines
Do beckon thee into the flickering wood,
Where moving spots of light show mystic flowers,
And wavering music fills the dreamy hours.

Summer Studies.

Hast thou no *time* for all this wondrous show,—
No thought to spare? Wilt thou forever be
With thy last year's dry flower-stalk and dead leaves,
And no new shoot or blossom on thy tree?

See how the pines push off their last year's leaves,
And stretch beyond them with exultant bound:

The grass and flowers, with living power, o'ergrow
Their last year's remnants on the greening ground.

Wilt thou, then, all thy wintry feelings keep,
The old dead routine of thy book-writ lore,
Nor deem that God can teach, by one bright hour,
What life hath never taught to thee before?

See what vast leisure, what unbounded rest,
Lie in the bending dome of the blue sky:
Ah! breathe that life-born languor from thy breast,
And know once more a child's unreasoning joy.

Cease, cease to *think*, and be content *to be;*
Swing safe at anchor in fair Nature's bay;
Reason no more, but o'er thy quiet soul
Let God's sweet teachings ripple their soft way.

Soar with the birds, and flutter with the leaf;
Dance with the seeded grass in fringy play;

Sail with the cloud, wave with the dreaming **pine**,
And float with Nature all the livelong day.

Call not such hours an idle waste **of time**, —
Land that lies fallow gains **a** quiet power;
It treasures, from the brooding of God's wings,
Strength to unfold the future tree and flower.

And when the summer's glorious **show is past,**
Its miracles no longer charm thy sight,
The treasured riches of those thoughtful hours
Shall make thy wintry **musings warm and bright.**

HOURS OF THE NIGHT;

OR,

WATCHES OF SORROW.

I.

MIDNIGHT.

"He hath made me to dwell in darkness as those that have been long dead."

ALL dark! — no light, no ray!
    Sun, moon, and stars, all gone!
Dimness of anguish! — utter void! —
    Crushed, and alone!

One waste of weary pain,
One dull, unmeaning ache,
A heart too weary even to throb,
    Too bruised to break.

No longer anxious thoughts,
No longer hopes and fears,
No strife, no effort, no desire,
　　No tears.

Daylight and leaves and flowers,
Summer and song of bird! —
All vanished! — dreams forever gone,
　　Unseen, unheard!

Love, beauty, youth, — all gone!
The high, heroic vow,
The buoyant hope, the fond desire, —
　　All ashes now!

The words they speak to me
Far off and distant seem,
As voices we have known and loved
　　Speak in a dream.

They bid me to submit;
I do, — I cannot strive;
I do not question, — I endure,
 Endure and live.

I do not struggle more,
Nor pray, for prayer is vain;
I but lie still the weary hour,
 And bear my pain.

A guiding God, a Friend,
A Father's gracious cheer,
Once seemed my own; but now even faith
 Lies buried here.

This darkened, deathly life
Is all remains of me,
And but one conscious wish, —
 To cease to be!

II.

FIRST HOUR.

"There was darkness over all the land from the sixth hour unto the ninth hour.

"And Jesus cried and said, My God, my God, why hast thou forsaken me?"

That cry hath stirred the deadness of my soul;
I feel a heart-string throb, as throbs a chord
When breaks the master chord of some great harp;
My heart responsive answers, "Why?" O Lord.

O cross of pain! O crown of cruel thorns!
O piercing nails! O spotless Sufferer there!
Wert *thou* forsaken in thy deadly strife?
Then canst thou pity me in my despair.

Take my dead heart, O Jesus, down with thee
To that still sepulchre where thou didst rest;
Lay it in the fair linen's spicy folds,
As a dear mother lays her babe to rest.

I am so worn, so weary, so o'erspent,
To lie with thee in that calm trance were sweet;
The bitter myrrh of long-remembered pain
May work in me new strength to rise again.

This dark and weary mystery of woe,
This hopeless struggle, this most useless strife, —
Ah, let it end! I die with thee, my Lord,
To all I ever hoped or wished from life.

I die with thee: thy fellowship of grief,
Thy partnership with mortal misery,
The weary watching and the nameless dread, —
Let them be mine to make me one with thee.

Thou hast asked, "Why?" and God will answer thee,
Therefore I ask not, but in peace lie down,
For the three days of mystery and rest,
Till comes the resurrection and the crown.

III.

SECOND HOUR.

"They laid hold upon one Simon a Cyrenian, and on him they laid the cross, that he might bear it after Jesus."

ALONG the dusty thoroughfare of life,
    Upon his daily errands walking free,
Came a brave, honest man, untouched by pain,
    Unchilled by sight or thought of misery.

But lo! a crowd: — he stops, — with curious eye
    A fainting form all pressed to earth he sees;
The hard, rough burden of the bitter cross
    Hath bowed the drooping head and feeble knees.

Ho! lay the cross upon yon stranger there,
    For he hath breadth of chest and strength of limb.
Straight it is done; and heavy laden thus,
    With Jesus' cross, he turns and follows him.

Unmurmuring, patient, cheerful, pitiful,
    Prompt with the holy sufferer to endure,
Forsaking all to follow the dear Lord, —
    Thus did he make his glorious calling sure.

O soul, whoe'er thou art, walking life's way,
    As yet from touch of deadly sorrow free,
Learn from this story to forecast the day
    When Jesus and his cross shall come to thee.

O, in that fearful, that decisive hour,
    Rebel not, shrink not, seek not thence to flee,
But, humbly bending, take thy heavy load,
    And bear it after Jesus patiently.

His cross is thine. If thou and he be one,
    Some portion of his pain must still be thine;
Thus only mayst thou share his glorious crown,
    And reign with him in majesty divine.

Master in sorrow! I accept my share
  In the great anguish of life's mystery.
No more, alone, I sink beneath my load,
  But bear my cross, O Jesus, after thee.

IV.

THIRD HOUR.

THE MYSTERY OF LIFE.

" Let my heart calm itself in thee. Let the great sea of my heart, that swelleth with waves, calm itself in thee."
STT. AUGUSTINE'S MANUAL.

LIFE'S mystery — deep, restless as the ocean —
    Hath surged and wailed for ages to and fro;
Earth's generations watch its ceaseless motion,
    As in and out its hollow moanings flow.
Shivering and yearning by that unknown sea,
Let my soul calm itself, O Christ, in thee!

Life's sorrows, with inexorable power,
    Sweep desolation o'er this mortal plain;
And human loves and hopes fly as the chaff
    Borne by the whirlwind from the ripened grain.
Ah! when before that blast my hopes all flee,
Let my soul calm itself, O Christ, in thee!

Between the mysteries of death and life
   Thou standest, loving, guiding, not explaining ;
We ask, and thou art silent ; yet we gaze,
   And our charmed hearts forget their drear complaining.
No crushing fate, no stony destiny,
O Lamb that hast been slain, we find in thee!

The many waves of thought, the mighty tides,
   The ground-swell that rolls up from other lands,
From far-off worlds, from dim, eternal shores,
   Whose echo dashes on life's wave-worn strands,
This vague, dark tumult of the inner sea
Grows calm, grows bright, O risen Lord, in thee !

Thy piercéd hand guides the mysterious wheels ;
   Thy thorn-crowned brow now wears the crown of power ;

And when the dread enigma presseth sore,
  Thy patient voice saith, "Watch with me one hour."
As sinks the moaning river in the sea
In silver peace, so sinks my soul in thee!

V.

FOURTH HOUR.

THE SORROWS OF MARY.

DEDICATED TO THE MOTHERS WHO HAVE LOST SONS IN THE LATE WAR.

I SLEPT, but my heart was waking,
    And out in my dreams I sped,
Through the streets of an ancient city,
    Where Jesus, the Lord, lay dead.

He was lying all cold and lowly,
　　And the sepulchre was sealed,
And the women that bore the spices
　　Had come from the holy field.

There is feasting in Pilate's palace,
　　There is revel in Herod's hall,
Where the lute and the sounding instrument
　　To mirth and merriment call.

"I have washed my hands," said Pilate,
　　"And what is the Jew to me?"
"I have missed my chance," said Herod,
　　"One of his wonders to see.

"But why should our courtly circle
　　To the thought give further place?
All dreams, save of pleasure and beauty,
　　Bid the dancers' feet efface."

　　＊　　　＊　　　＊　　　＊

I saw a light from a casement,
　　And entered a lowly door,
Where a woman, stricken and mournful,
　　Sat in sackcloth on the floor.

There Mary, the mother of Jesus,
　　And John, the belovéd one,
With a few poor friends beside them,
　　Were mourning for Him that was gone.

And before the mother was lying
　　That crown of cruel thorn,
Wherewith they crowned that gentle brow
　　In mockery that morn.

And her ears yet ring with the anguish
　　Of that last dying cry, —
That mighty appeal of agony
　　That shook both earth and sky.

O God, what a shaft of anguish
    Was that dying voice from the tree! —
From Him the only spotless, —
    "Why hast Thou forsaken me?"

And was he of God forsaken?
    They ask, appalled with dread;
Is evil crowned and triumphant,
    And goodness vanquished and dead?

Is there, then, no God in Jacob?
    Is the star of Judah dim?
For who would our God deliver,
    If he would not deliver him?

If God *could* not deliver, — what hope then?
    If he *would* not, — who ever shall dare
To be firm in his service hereafter?
    To trust in his wisdom or care?

So darkly the Tempter was saying,
  To hearts that with sorrow were dumb,
And the poor souls were clinging in **darkness to**
    God,
  With hands that with anguish were numb.

    *   *   *   *   *

In my dreams came the third day morning,
  And fairly the **day-star shone;**
But fairer, the solemn angel,
  As he rolled away the stone.

In the lowly dwelling of Mary,
  In the dusky twilight chill,
There was heard the sound of coming feet,
  And her very heart grew still.

And in the glimmer of dawning,
  She saw him enter the door,
Her Son, all living and real,
  Risen, to die no more!

Her Son, all living and real,
    Risen no more to die, —
With the power of an endless life in his face,
    With the light of heaven in his eye.

O mourning mothers, so many,
    Weeping o'er sons that are dead,
Have ye thought of the sorrows of Mary's heart,
    Of the tears that Mary shed?

Is the crown of thorns before you?
    Are there memories of cruel scorn?
Of hunger and thirst and bitter cold
    That your beloved have borne?

Had ye ever a son like Jesus
    To give to a death of pain?
Did ever a son so cruelly die,
    But did he die in vain?

Have ye ever thought that all the hopes
 That make our earth-life fair
Were born in those three bitter days
 Of Mary's deep despair?

O mourning mothers, so many,
 Weeping in woe and pain,
Think on the joy of Mary's heart
 In a Son that is risen again.

Have faith in a third-day morning,
 In a resurrection-hour;
For what ye sow in weakness,
 He can raise again in power.

Have faith in the Lord of that thorny crown,
 In the Lord of the piercéd hand;
For he reigneth now o'er earth and heaven,
 And his power who may withstand?

And the hopes that never on earth shall bloom,
The sorrows forever new,
Lay silently down at the feet of Him
Who died and is risen for you.

VI.

DAY DAWN.

THE dim gray dawn, upon the eastern hills,
    Brings back to light once more the cheer-
        less scene;
But oh! no morning in my Father's house
    Is dawning now, for there no night hath been.

Ten thousand thousand now, on Zion's hills,
    All robed in white, with palmy crowns, do stray,
While I, an exile, far from fatherland,
    Still wandering, faint along the desert way.

O home! dear home! my own, my native home!
O Father, friends! when shall I look on you?
When shall these weary wanderings be o'er,
And I be gathered back to stray no more?

O Thou, the brightness of whose gracious face
These weary, longing eyes have never seen, —
By whose dear thought, for whose belovéd sake,
My course, through toil and tears, I daily take, —

I think of thee when the myrrh-dropping morn
    Steps forth upon the purple eastern steep ;
I think of thee in the fair eventide,
    When the bright-sandalled stars their watches keep.

And trembling hope, and fainting, sorrowing love,
    On thy dear word for comfort doth rely ;
And clear-eyed Faith, with strong forereaching gaze,
    Beholds thee here, unseen, but ever nigh.

Walking in white with thee, she dimly sees,
    All beautiful, these lovely ones withdrawn,
With whom my heart went upward, as they rose,
    Like morning stars, to light a coming dawn.

All sinless now, and crowned and glorified,
  Where'er thou movest move they still with thee.
As erst, in sweet communion by thy side,
  Walked John and Mary in old Galilee.

But hush, my heart! 'T is but a day or two
  Divides thee from that bright, immortal shore.
Rise up! rise up! and gird thee for the race!
  Fast fly the hours, and all will soon be o'er.

Thou hast the new name written in thy soul;
  Thou hast the mystic stone He gives his own.
Thy soul, made one with him, shall feel no more
  That she is walking on her path alone.

VII.

WHEN I AWAKE I AM STILL WITH THEE.

STILL, still with Thee, when purple morning breaketh,
   When the bird waketh and the shadows flee;
Fairer than morning, lovelier than the daylight,
   Dawns the sweet consciousness, *I am with Thee!*

Alone with Thee, amid the mystic shadows,
   The solemn hush of nature newly born;
Alone with Thee in breathless adoration,
   In the calm dew and freshness of the morn.

As in the dawning o'er the waveless ocean
   The image of the morning star doth rest,
So in this stillness Thou beholdest only
   Thine image in the waters of my breast.

When I awake I am still with Thee.

Still, still with Thee! as to each new-born morning
  A fresh and solemn splendor still is given,
So doth this blessed consciousness, awaking,
  Breathe, each day, nearness unto Thee and heaven.

When sinks the soul, subdued by toil, to slumber,
  Its closing eye looks up to Thee in prayer;
Sweet the repose beneath the wings o'ershading,
  But sweeter still to wake and find Thee there.

So shall it be at last, in that bright morning
  When the soul waketh and life's shadows flee;
O, in that hour, fairer than daylight dawning,
  Shall rise the glorious thought, *I am with Thee!*

PRESSED FLOWERS FROM ITALY.

A DAY

IN THE

PAMFILI DORIA.

A DAY IN THE PAMFILI DORIA.

THOUGH the hills are cold and snowy,
   And the wind drives chill to-day,
My heart goes back to a spring-time,
   Far, far in the past away.

And I see a quaint old city,
   Weary and worn and brown,
Where the spring and the birds are so early,
   And the sun in such light goes down.

I remember that old-times villa,
   Where our afternoons went by,
Where the suns of March flushed warmly,
   And spring was in earth and sky.

Out of the mouldering city,
  Mouldering, old, and gray,
We sped, with a lightsome heart-thrill,
  For a sunny, gladsome day, —

For a revel of fresh spring verdure,
  For a race 'mid springing flowers,
For a vision of plashing fountains,
  Of birds and blossoming bowers.

There were violet banks in the shadows,
  Violets white and blue;
And a world of bright anemones,
  That over the terrace grew, —

Blue and orange and purple,
  Rosy and yellow and white,
Rising in rainbow bubbles,
  Streaking the lawns with light.

And down from the old stone pine-trees,
   Those far off islands of air,
The birds are flinging the tidings
   Of a joyful revel up there.

And now for the grand old fountains,
   Tossing their silvery spray,
Those fountains so quaint and so **many,**
   That are leaping and singing all day.

Those fountains of strange weird sculpture,
   With lichens and moss o'ergrown,
Are they marble greening in moss-wreaths?
   Or moss-wreaths whitening to stone?

Down many a wild, dim pathway
   We ramble from morning till noon;
We linger, unheeding the hours,
   Till evening comes all too soon.

And from out the ilex alleys,
  Where lengthening shadows play,
We look on the dreamy Campagna,
  All glowing with setting day, —

All melting in bands of purple,
  In swathings and foldings of gold,
In ribands of azure and lilac,
  Like a princely banner unrolled.

And the smoke of each distant cottage,
  And the flash of each villa white,
Shines out with an opal glimmer,
  Like gems in a casket of light.

And the dome of old St. Peter's
  With a strange translucence glows,
Like a mighty bubble of amethyst
  Floating in waves of rose.

A Day in the Pamfili Doria.

In a trance of dreamy vagueness
   We, gazing and yearning, behold
That city beheld by the prophet,
   Whose walls were transparent gold.

And, dropping all solemn and slowly,
   To hallow the softening spell,
There falls on the dying twilight
   The Ave Maria bell.

With a mournful motherly softness,
   With a weird and weary care,
That strange and ancient city
   Seems calling the nations to prayer.

And the words that of old the angel
   To the mother of Jesus brought,
Rise like a new evangel,
   To hallow the trance of our thought.

With the smoke of the evening incense,
    Our thoughts are ascending then
To Mary, the mother of Jesus,
    To Jesus, the Master of men.

O city of prophets and martyrs,
    O shrines of the sainted dead,
When, when shall the living day-spring
    Once more on your towers be spread?

When He who is meek and lowly
    Shall rule in those lordly halls,
And shall stand and feed as a shepherd
    The flock which his mercy calls, —

O, then to those noble churches,
    To picture and statue and gem,
To the pageant of solemn worship,
    Shall the *meaning* come back again.

And this strange and ancient city,

   In that reign of His truth **and** love,

Shall *be* what it *seems* in the twilight,

   The type of that City above.

THE GARDENS OF THE VATICAN.

SWEET fountains, plashing with a dreamy fall,
    And mosses green, and tremulous veils of fern,
And banks of blowing cyclamen, and stars,
Blue as the skies, of myrtle blossoming,
The twilight shade of ilex overhead
O'erbubbling with sweet song of nightingale,
With walks of strange, weird stillness, leading on
'Mid sculptured fragments half to green moss gone,
Or breaking forth amid the violet leaves
With some white gleam of an old world gone by.
Ah! strange, sweet quiet! wilderness of calm,
Gardens of dreamy rest, I long to lay
Beneath your shade the last long sigh, and say,
Here is my home, my Lord, thy home and mine;

And I, having searched the world with many a tear,
At last have found thee and will stray no more.
But vainly here I seek the Gardener
That Mary saw. These lovely halls beyond,
That airy, sky-like dome, that lofty fane,
Is as a palace whence the king is gone
And taken all the sweetness with himself.
Turn again, Jesus, and possess thine own!
Come to thy temple once more as of old!
Drive forth the money-changers, let it be
A house of prayer for nations. Even so,
    Amen! Amen!

ST. PETER'S CHURCH.

HOLY WEEK, APRIL, 1860.

O FAIREST mansion of a Father's love,
Harmonious! hospitable! with thine arms
Outspread to all, thy fountains ever full,
And, fair as heaven, thy misty, sky-like dome
Hung like the firmament with circling sweep
Above the constellated golden lamps
That burn forever round the holy tomb.
Most meet art thou to be the Father's house,
The house of prayer for nations. Come the time
When thou shalt be so! when a liberty,
Wide as thine arms, high as thy lofty dome,
Shall be proclaimed, by thy loud singing choirs,
Like voice of many waters! Then the Lord
Shall come into his temple, and make pure

The sons of Levi ; then, as once of old,

The blind shall see, the lame leap as an hart,

And to the poor the Gospel shall be preached.

And Easter's **silver-sounding** trumpets tell,

"The Lord is risen indeed," to die no more.

Hasten it in **its time.** Amen! Amen!

THE MISERERE.

NOT of the earth that music! all things fade;
Vanish the pictured walls! and, one by one,
The starry candles silently expire!

And now, O Jesus! round that silent cross
A moment's pause, a hush as of the grave.
Now rises slow a silver mist of sound,
And all the heavens break out in drops of grief;
A rain of sobbing sweetness, swelling, dying,
Voice into voice inweaving with sweet throbs,
And fluttering pulses of impassioned moan,—
Veiled voices, in whose wailing there is awe,
And mysteries of love and agony,
A yearning anguish of celestial souls,

A shiver as of wings trembling the air,
As if God's shining doves, his spotless birds,
Wailed with a nightingale's heart-break of grief,
In this their starless night, when for our sins
Their sun, their life, their love, hangs darkly there,
Like a slain lamb, bleeding his life away!

www.ingramcontent.com/pod-product-compliance
Lightning Source LLC
Chambersburg PA
CBHW020145170426
43199CB00010B/896